Attainment's
Early Literacy Skills Builder

Assessment Manual

Level 1
Level A

Diane Browder
Susan Gibbs
Lynn Ahlgrim-Delzell
Ginevra Courtade
Angel Lee

Early Literacy Skills Builder (ELSB) Assessment Manual
Levels 1 and A

Diane Browder • Susan Gibbs • Lynn Ahlgrim-Delzell • Ginevra Courtade • Angel Lee

Editing Linda Schreiber
Cover design Beverly Sanders
Cover illustration Jo Reynolds
Graphic design Elizabeth Ragsdale

ISBN: 1-57861-917-3
An Attainment Publication
© 2007, Revised Edition 2016, Attainment Company, Inc.
All rights reserved.
Printed in the United States of America

Attainment Company, Inc.
PO Box 930160
Verona, WI 53593-0160
1-800-327-4269
www.AttainmentCompany.com

Contents

Overview 4

Level 1 6
Objective 1   Read sight words using time-delay instruction. 7
Objective 2   Point to sight words to complete sentences. 17
Objective 3   Point to text as it is read 47
Objective 4   Say and/or point to a word to complete a repeated story line 61
Objective 5   Respond to literal questions about a story. 83
Objective 8   Identify letter-sound correspondences. 97
Objective 13   Point to pictures/words representing new vocabulary 107

Level A 116
Objective 1   Recognize a book from a nonbook 117
Objective 2   Interact with objects related to a book 121
Objective 3   Select own photo or written name 123
Objective 4   Select named photo or word. 127
Objective 5   Physically engage with a book and/or visually attend to a story 138
Objective 6   Point to an object, a picture, or a word that completes a story line . 143
Objective 7   Respond to literal questions about a story. 151
Objective 8   Point to named objects or pictures 162

Overview

The **Level 1 or Level A Assessment** should be administered at the completion of Level 1 or Level A to determine when a student is ready to move on to the next level of the curriculum. Test items measure mastery of the objectives taught in each level of the **Early Literacy Skills Builder (ELSB)** curriculum.

Preparation

Preparing for the administration of the assessment is easy:

- Practice the script for administering the assessment items before administering the assessment. Specific instructions for administering each item of the assessment appear opposite the response page for the student.
- Prepare for the student's mode of response if different from traditional pointing or speaking, and decide if you will need to modify the directions to accommodate the response mode.
- Prepare a **Recording Form** for the level being assessed.
- Use 2" × 2" Post-it® notes to cover the yellow highlighted words for Objective 4 in Level 1 and Objective 6 in Level A.
- In Level 1, for Objective 2, have available the sight word flashcards: boy, girl, friend, and green.
- Have the **All About Moe** easel book with the stories "Hello, Moe," and "Moe Likes to Sing" available for assessment of Objective 5 in Level 1, and the **Oh My, Apple Pie!** easel book for Level A.
- If administering Level A of the assessment, you will also need the following materials:
  - Sock
  - Red and green apples
  - Photo of student and photo of person unfamiliar to student
  - Book
  - Index cards
  - Orange
  - Pencil

Mode of Response and Modifications

Students with significant disabilities may need individualized modes of responding, such as pointing, grasping, or eye gaze. It is important that the mode of responding is consistent for both assessment and instruction of skills. The ELSB curriculum and assessment can be delivered using any response mode that can be conceived of by modifying the materials and the directions. Materials can be modified by printing them from Disc 1. They can be enlarged, laminated, cut apart, and/or adhered to eye gaze boards or augmentative or alternative communication (AAC) devices. If using AAC devices, the responses should be preprogrammed. It is also appropriate to modify the directions in the assessment, for example, changing "Point to" to "Give me," "Look at," or "Touch."

Allowable Verbal Prompts

Verbal prompts can be given only once. The prompt can be given after 5 seconds without a response. The allowable verbal prompts are given following the item direction.

Recording Forms

Reproducible Recording Forms for noting the student's responses for Levels 1 and A are included in Appendix E of the ELSB Implementation Guide. They are also included on Disc 1 for convenient printing. Note that the Recording Form allows you to enter information over time. The student responses on initial administration are recorded on the form under the Test 1 column and under the appropriate column for subsequent administrations of the assessment.

Using the Assessment to Determine Mastery

Administer the assessment to determine an individual student's level of mastery. Administer each level's test once the student has completed Lesson 5. For each objective, total the number of items that were correctly performed independently (without prompting) and transfer the total to the Assessment Summary on the cover of the Recording Form. Add the total for each objective for a total level score. Divide the number of items correct by the total number of possible correct items. Multiply by 100 to determine the percent of correct responses performed independently for the level.

The recommended percentage for mastery of a level is 75% or greater. This percentage can be revised depending on a given student's needs. Higher percentages correct indicate a greater level of mastery. If a student reaches the level of mastery, it is appropriate to advance the student to the next level of ELSB. If a student does not reach mastery, there are three options:

1. Repeat the level, perhaps going at a faster pace, but reviewing all of the objectives. Then, re-administer the assessment to redetermine mastery.

2. Reteach selected objectives for which the student had difficulty. Then re-administer the assessment.

3. Advance the student to the next level, but monitor the student's progress. Many of the skills spiral through the curriculum and are addressed again in upper levels. If a specific skill is preventing the student from progressing, it is possible to continue on through the curriculum while addressing the objective with extra instruction at other times of the day.

Refer to the ELSB Implementation Guide for additional information on working with students who do not achieve mastery.

Level 1

Objective 1

Read sight words using time-delay instruction

dog   Moe   is

Demonstration Directions

Say, **I will find a word. Like this, Moe.** Touch the word *Moe*. Say, **Now you try it. Find the word Moe.** Allow 5 seconds for the student to initiate a response. If no response or an incorrect response, encourage the student to respond. Say, **Like this,** and repeat touching the word *Moe* and directing the student to find it.

boy   **friend**

Administration Directions

Present the student page to the student. Then say, **Point to *boy*.** Pause for 5 seconds, waiting for the student to initiate a response.

Allowable Verbal Prompt

Which one is *boy*?

friend   boy

Administration Directions

Present the student page to the student. Then say, **Point to *friend*.** Pause for 5 seconds, waiting for the student to initiate a response.

Allowable Verbal Prompt

Which one is *friend*?

boy   friend   girl

Administration Directions

Present the student page to the student. Then say, **Point to *girl*.** Pause for 5 seconds, waiting for the student to initiate a response.

Allowable Verbal Prompt

Which one is *girl*?

Objective 2

Point to sight words to complete sentences

Moe is a green frog.

Demonstration Directions

Say, **Now I'm going to read words in a sentence. Listen.** Read the sentence, pointing to each word as you read. Turn the page.

Moe is a _____ frog.

Materials

Sight word flashcards: girl, friend, green

Demonstration Directions

Say, **See, here is the sentence. It has a word missing. Which word goes here?** Read the sentence again, pointing to each word. Pause at the blank space, and then say the last word. Present the *green* flashcard and one of the sight word flashcards and say, **Point to the word that goes here.** Do not label the word choices. If no response or an incorrect response, encourage the student to respond by saying, **Like this,** and then point to *green,* the correct word. Say, **Green is the missing word. Moe is a green frog.** Repeat the request to find the missing word.

Moe is a <u>boy</u> frog.

Administration Directions

Say, **Listen.** Read the sentence, pointing to each word as you read. Turn the page.

Moe is a _____ frog.

Materials

Sight word flashcards: boy, girl, friend

Administration Directions

Say, **Which word goes here?** Point to the blank space. **Listen.** Read the sentence and point to the words. Pause at the blank space, and then say the last word. Present a sight word flashcard and the *boy* flashcard and say, **Point to the word that goes here.**

Allowable Verbal Prompt

Which one? _____ or *boy?*

Leonard is a <u>boy</u>.

Administration Directions

Say, **Listen.** Read the sentence, pointing to each word as you read. Turn the page.

Leonard is a _____.

Materials

Sight word flashcards: boy, girl, friend

Administration Directions

Say, **Which word goes here?** Point to the blank space. **Listen.** Read the sentence and point to the words. Pause at the blank space. Present a sight word flashcard and the *boy* flashcard and say, **Point to the word that goes here.**

Allowable Verbal Prompt

Which one? *Boy* **or _____?**

Moe is your friend.

Administration Directions

Say, **Listen.** Read the sentence, pointing to each word as you read. Turn the page.

Moe is your _____.

Materials

Sight word flashcards: boy, girl, friend

Administration Directions

Say, **Which word goes here?** Point to the blank space. **Listen.** Read the sentence and point to the words. Pause at the blank space. Present a sight word flashcard and the *friend* flashcard and say, **Point to the word that goes here.**

Allowable Verbal Prompt

Which one? _____ or *friend*?

My dog is my friend.

Administration Directions

Say, **Listen.** Read the sentence, pointing to each word as you read. Turn the page.

My dog is my _____.

Materials

Sight word flashcards: boy, girl, friend

Administration Directions

Say, **Which word goes here?** Point to the blank space. **Listen.** Read the sentence and point to the words. Pause at the blank space. Present a sight word flashcard and the *friend* flashcard and say, **Point to the word that goes here.**

Allowable Verbal Prompt

Which one? _____ or *friend?*

My sister is a girl.

Administration Directions

Say, **Listen.** Read the sentence, pointing to each word as you read. Turn the page.

My sister is a _____.

Materials

Sight word flashcards: boy, girl, friend

Administration Directions

Say, **Which word goes here?** Point to the blank space. **Listen.** Read the sentence and point to the words. Pause at the blank space. Present a sight word flashcard and the *girl* flashcard and say, **Point to the word that goes here.**

Allowable Verbal Prompt

Which one? *Girl* **or _____?**

Sally is a <u>girl</u>.

Administration Directions

Say, **Listen.** Read the sentence, pointing to each word as you read. Turn the page.

Sally is a _____.

Materials

Sight word flashcards: boy, girl, friend

Administration Directions

Say, **Which word goes here?** Point to the blank space. **Listen.** Read the sentence and point to the words. Pause at the blank space. Present a sight word flashcard and the *girl* flashcard and say, **Point to the word that goes here.**

Allowable Verbal Prompt

Which one? _____ or *girl*?

Objective 3

Point to text as it is read

Molly is a happy frog.

Demonstration Directions

Say, **See this sentence? I will point to the words as I read. Like this.** Read the line, dragging your finger along as you read each word. Say, **Now you try it. Point to the words as I read.** Provide a prompt by pointing to the first word. Allow 5 seconds for the student to initiate a response. If no response, encourage the student by saying, **Like this,** and repeat by reading and dragging your finger along as you read. Slow the rate of reading to accommodate students who physically move slower. For all Objective 3 items, count movement left-to-right as correct. Students do not need to touch word-for-word at this level.

Allowable Verbal Prompt

Point to all the words.

Moe is a green frog.

Administration Directions

While the student is viewing the sentence, point to the first word and say, **Point to the words as I read.** Pause for 5 seconds to wait for the student to initiate a response. Slow the rate of reading to accommodate students who physically move slower.

Allowable Verbal Prompt

Point to all the words.

Moe can jump.

Administration Directions

While the student is viewing the sentence, point to the first word and say, **Point to the words as I read.** Pause for 5 seconds to wait for the student to initiate a response. Slow the rate of reading to accommodate students who physically move slower.

Allowable Verbal Prompt

Point to all the words.

Moe is a green frog.

Moe is a boy frog.

Administration Directions

While the student is viewing the sentences, point to the first word and say, **Point to the words as I read.** Pause for 5 seconds to wait for the student to initiate a response. Slow the rate of reading to accommodate students who physically move slower.

Allowable Verbal Prompt

Point to all the words.

Moe can sing.

Moe can sing.

Administration Directions

While the student is viewing the sentences, point to the first word and say, **Point to the words as I read.** Pause for 5 seconds to wait for the student to initiate a response. Slow the rate of reading to accommodate students who physically move slower.

Allowable Verbal Prompt

Point to all the words.

I am at school, and I can say,

"Ribbit, ribbit, ribbit!"

Administration Directions

While the student is viewing the sentence, point to the first word and say, **Point to the words as I read.** Pause for 5 seconds to wait for the student to initiate a response. Slow the rate of reading to accommodate students who physically move slower.

Allowable Verbal Prompt

Point to all the words.

Objective 4

Say and/or point to a word to complete a repeated story line

Moe is a green frog.

Moe is a **green** frog.

| green | chair |

Note: For this demonstration and items 15–18, cover the word highlighted in yellow on the student page with a Post-it® note. If the student is nonverbal, preprogram an AAC device to say the repeated word for the demonstration item and items 15–18. Have the AAC device accessible to the student before reading the sentences so you can see if the student is anticipating the hidden word.

Demonstration Directions

Say, **I'm going to read sentences and say a hidden word. Then I'll point to the word down here. Like this.** Read the sentences, pointing to the words. Say *green* as you uncover the hidden word. (If using an AAC device, hit the button each time you read the word *green*.) Then touch below the word *green* and say, **Here is the word *green*. You try it. Tell me the hidden word and find the word down here.** Replace the Post-it® note. Read the line with the hidden word again. If no response or an incorrect response, encourage the student by saying, **Like this.** Then repeat by covering the word again, touching below the word *green*, and directing the student to point to it and say it (or use the AAC device).

Moe is your friend.

Moe is your **friend**.

| friend | chair |

Administration Directions

Say, **I'm going to read these sentences. Tell me the hidden word and find the word down here.** Read each line, pointing to the words. Pause at the hidden word. Uncover the word as the student says (or uses the AAC device to say) the hidden word. Allow 5 seconds for the student to initiate saying the word and pointing to it before moving on to the next item.

Allowable Verbal Prompts

Tell me the hidden word or **Point to the hidden word.**

He can jump over a book.

He can **jump** under a table.

| desk | jump |

Administration Directions

Say, **I'm going to read these sentences. Tell me the hidden word and find the word down here.** Read each line, pointing to the words. Pause at the hidden word. Uncover the word as the student says (or uses the AAC device to say) the hidden word. Allow 5 seconds for the student to initiate saying the word and pointing to it before moving on to the next item.

Allowable Verbal Prompts

Tell me the hidden word or **Point to the hidden word.**

Moe is a green frog.

Moe is a boy frog.

| flower | frog |

Administration Directions

Say, **I'm going to read these sentences. Tell me the hidden word and find the word down here.** Read each line, pointing to the words. Pause at the hidden word. Uncover the word as the student says (or uses the AAC device to say) the hidden word. Allow 5 seconds for the student to initiate saying the word and pointing to it before moving on to the next item.

Allowable Verbal Prompts

Tell me the hidden word or **Point to the hidden word.**

Moe can sing.

Moe can sing.

| sing | hammer |

Administration Directions

Say, **I'm going to read these sentences. Tell me the hidden word and find the word down here.** Read each line, pointing to the words. Pause at the hidden word. Uncover the word as the student says (or uses the AAC device to say) the hidden word. Allow 5 seconds for the student to initiate saying the word and pointing to it before moving on to the next item.

Allowable Verbal Prompts

Tell me the hidden word or **Point to the hidden word.**

Moe is a <mark>green</mark> frog.

green	chair

Note: This portion of Objective 4 provides picture representation of the word. For this demonstration and items 19–22, cover the word highlighted in yellow on the student page with a Post-it® note.

Demonstration Directions

Say, **I'm going to read this sentence and point to a picture of the hidden word down here. Like this.** Read the sentence, pointing to the words. Point to *green* as you uncover the hidden word. Point to the green square at the bottom of the page and say *green.* Replace the Post-it® note. Say, **You try it.** Reread the sentence while pointing to the words. Say, **Point to *green*** when you uncover the hidden word. If no response or an incorrect response, encourage the student by saying, **Like this,** and repeat pointing to the green square.

Moe is your **friend**.

| friend | chair |

Administration Directions

Read the sentence while pointing to the words. Stop at the hidden word and uncover it. Say, **Point to *friend.*** Allow 5 seconds for the student to initiate a response before moving on to the next item. If the student selects the incorrect word before you finish reading the sentence, score as incorrect. Put your hand over the picture and say, **Wait until I am finished,** and repeat the direction. This prompt may be provided once.

Allowable Verbal Prompt

Point to *friend.*

He can **jump** under a table.

| desk | jump |

Administration Directions

Read the sentence while pointing to the words. Stop at the hidden word and uncover it. Say, **Point to *jump*.** Allow 5 seconds for the student to initiate a response before moving on to the next item. If the student selects the incorrect word before you finish reading the sentence, score as incorrect. Put your hand over the picture and say, **Wait until I am finished,** and repeat the direction. This prompt may be provided once.

Allowable Verbal Prompt

Point to *jump*.

Moe is a boy ==frog==.

| flower | frog |

Administration Directions

Read the sentence while pointing to the words. Stop at the hidden word and uncover it. Say, **Point to *frog*.** Allow 5 seconds for the student to initiate a response before moving on to the next item. If the student selects the incorrect word before you finish reading the sentence, score as incorrect. Put your hand over the picture and say, **Wait until I am finished,** and repeat the direction. This prompt may be provided once.

Allowable Verbal Prompt

Point to *frog*.

Moe can sing.

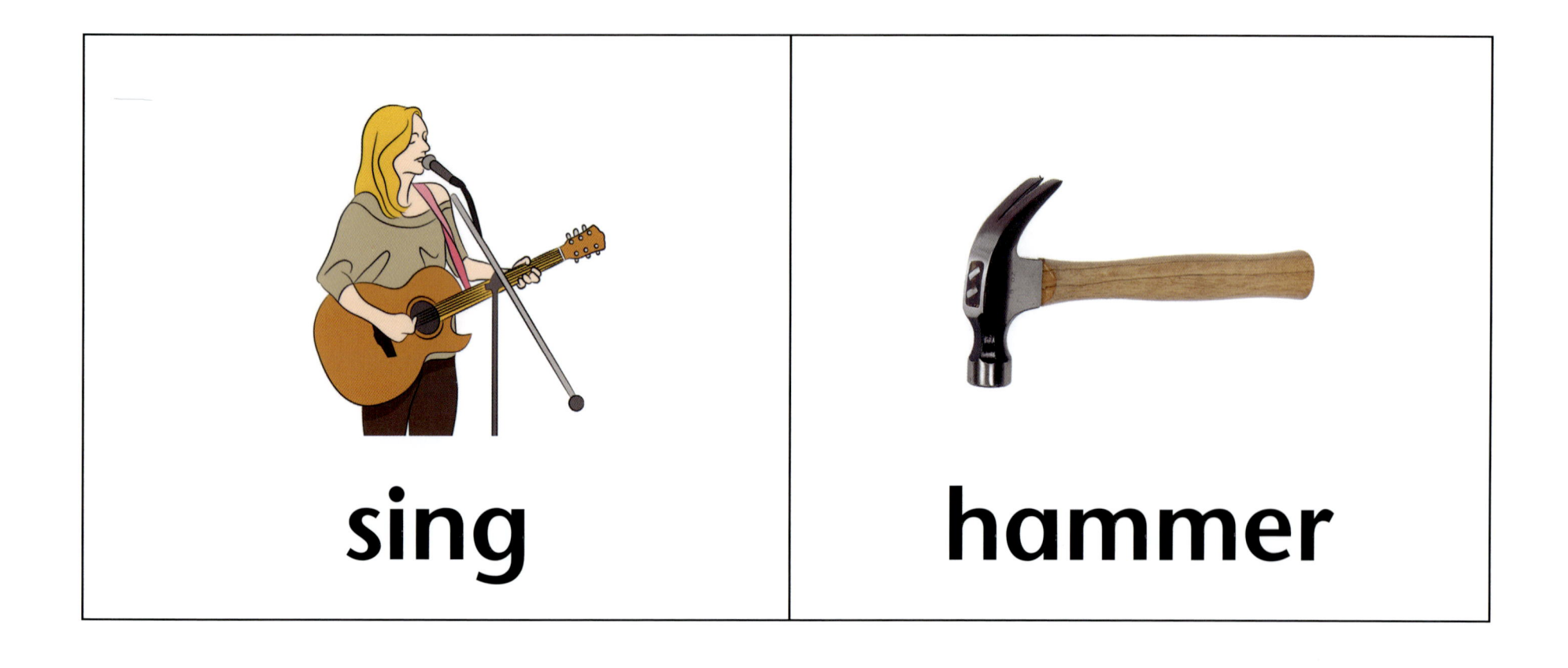

| sing | hammer |

Administration Directions

Read the sentence while pointing to the words. Stop at the hidden word and uncover it. Say, **Point to *sing*.** Allow 5 seconds for the student to initiate a response before moving on to the next item. If the student selects the incorrect word before you finish reading the sentence, score as incorrect. Put your hand over the picture and say, **Wait until I am finished,** and repeat the direction. This prompt may be provided once.

Allowable Verbal Prompt

Point to *sing*.

Objective 5

Respond to literal questions about a story

frog

book

> **Note:** You will need the **All About Moe** easel book with the "Hello, Moe" and "Moe Likes to Sing" stories for this objective.

Administration Directions

Display the "Hello, Moe" story so the student can see it. While you read the story, drag your finger along below the words. Ask the question immediately after reading the line where the answer appears.

What is Moe? (Line 1)

Allowable Verbal Prompts

Repeat the question or ask, **Which one? A frog or a book?**

friend

shoe

Administration Directions

Display the "Hello, Moe" story so the student can see it. While you read the story, drag your finger along below the words. Ask the question immediately after reading the line where the answer appears.

Who is Moe? (Line 3)

Allowable Verbal Prompts

Repeat the question or ask, **Which one? Friend or shoe?**

jump

run

Administration Directions

Display the "Hello, Moe" story so the student can see it. While you read the story, drag your finger along below the words. Ask the question immediately after reading the line where the answer appears.

What can Moe do? (Line 4)

Allowable Verbal Prompts

Repeat the question or ask, **Which one? Jump or run?**

girls

turtles

Administration Directions

Display the "Moe Likes to Sing" story so the student can see it. While you read the story, drag your finger along below the words. Ask the question immediately after reading the line where the answer appears.

Moe likes boys. Who else does Moe like?
(Line 4)

Allowable Verbal Prompts

Repeat the question or ask, **Which ones? Girls or turtles?**

forks

sing

Administration Directions

Display the "Moe Likes to Sing" story so the student can see it. While you read the story, drag your finger along below the words. Ask the question immediately after reading the line where the answer appears.

What can Moe do? (Line 6)

Allowable Verbal Prompts

Repeat the question or ask, **Which one? Forks or sing?**

| **Ribbit, ribbit, ribbit.** | **Meow, meow, meow.** |

Administration Directions

Display the "Moe Likes to Sing" story so the student can see it. While you read the story, drag your finger along below the words. Ask the question immediately after reading the line where the answer appears.

What can Moe say? (Line 11)

Allowable Verbal Prompts

Repeat the question or ask, **Which one? Ribbit or meow?**

Objective 8

Identify letter-sound correspondences

Objective 8: Demonstration

f

Note: Remember to say the sound the letter makes when the sound is written within the virgules. Do not add a vowel sound (e.g., /f/ not /fuh/). Stretch the sound when multiple letters appear.

Demonstration Directions

Say, **This letter says the sound /fff/. Touch the letter that makes the /fff/ sound.** After 5 seconds, if no response, say, **Like this. Point to the letter. Now you do it. Touch the letter that makes the /fff/ sound.**

Objective 8: Item 29 • 100

m

Administration Directions

Say, **Touch the letter that makes the /mmm/ sound.** After 5 seconds, if no response repeat, **Touch the letter that makes the /mmm/ sound.**

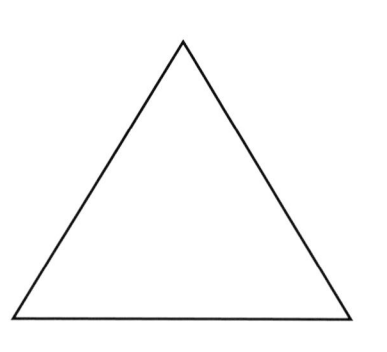

Objective 8: Item 30 • 102

m

Administration Directions

Say, **Touch the letter that makes the /mmm/ sound.** After 5 seconds, if no response repeat, **Touch the letter that makes the /mmm/ sound.**

m

Administration Directions

Say, **Touch the letter that makes the /mmm/ sound.** After 5 seconds, if no response repeat, **Touch the letter that makes the /mmm/ sound.**

Objective 13

Point to pictures/words representing new vocabulary

bird

sun

sing

tree

Demonstration Directions

Say, **We are going to find some words, like *sing*.** Point to *sing* and pause for 5 seconds for student to initiate a response. If no response or an incorrect response, say, **This is *sing*. Now you point to *sing*.**

flower	**boy**
candy	**bear**

Administration Directions

Say, **Your turn. Point to *boy*.** Note: If the student selects the wrong word before you finish giving the direction, score it as incorrect. However, provide the student with an opportunity to learn to wait for the full direction. Prompt waiting behavior by putting your hand over the page and saying, **Wait until I am finished. Point to *boy*.**

Allowable Verbal Prompt

Point to *boy*.

friend

dog

bus

drum

Administration Directions

Say, **Your turn. Point to *friend*.** Note: If the student selects the wrong word before you finish giving the direction, score it as incorrect. However, provide the student with an opportunity to learn to wait for the full direction. Prompt waiting behavior by putting your hand over the page and saying, **Wait until I am finished. Point to *friend*.**

Allowable Verbal Prompt

Point to *friend*.

rat	girl
bee	socks

Administration Directions

Say, **Your turn. Point to *girl*.** Note: If the student selects the wrong word before you finish giving the direction, score it as incorrect. However, provide the student with an opportunity to learn to wait for the full direction. Prompt waiting behavior by putting your hand over the page and saying, **Wait until I am finished. Point to *girl*.**

Allowable Verbal Prompt

Point to *girl*.

Level A

Objective 1

Recognize a book from a nonbook

Materials

Oh My, Apple Pie! easel book

Administration Directions

Hold the book out for the student to see and say, **This book is called Oh My, Apple Pie! Look at our book.** Allow 5 seconds for the student to initiate a looking response. Wait as long as it takes for the student to complete the response. If no response after 5 seconds, encourage the student to look by tapping on or shaking the book and using the prompt.

Substitutions

Depending upon the language repertoire and physical ability of the student, substitute the words *touch* or *show me* for *look at*.

Allowable Verbal Prompts

Look at the apple pie on the cover of our book.

Materials

- **Oh My, Apple Pie!** easel book
- A sock

Administration Directions

Present the book and a sock (as a distractor). Say, **This is a book** (attract attention to the book by shaking it or tapping it), **and this is a sock** (attract attention to the sock by shaking it or tapping it). **Which one is the book?** Allow 5 seconds for the student to initiate a response. Wait as long as it takes for the student to complete the response.

Substitutions

Depending upon the language repertoire and physical ability of the student, substitute the words *touch, look at,* or *show me* for *Which one is . . .?*

Allowable Verbal Prompt

Which one is the book?

Materials

- **Oh My, Apple Pie!** easel book
- Another book

Administration Directions

Present the Oh My, Apple Pie! book and another book as a distractor. Say, **Here are two books. Which book is Oh My, Apple Pie? It has an apple pie on the cover.** Allow 5 seconds for the student to initiate a response. Wait as long as it takes for the student to complete the response.

Substitutions

Depending upon the language repertoire and physical ability of the student, substitute the words *touch, look at,* or *show me* for *Which one is . . .?*

Allowable Verbal Prompt

Which book is Oh My, Apple Pie?

Objective 2

Interact with objects related to a book

Materials

- **Oh My, Apple Pie!** easel book, p. 2
- A red apple

Administration Directions

Present the apple and say, **Here is an apple just like the one on this page of our book. Touch the apple.** Allow 5 seconds for the student to initiate a response. Wait as long as it takes for the student to complete the response.

Substitutions

Depending upon the language repertoire and physical ability of the student, substitute the words *look at* or *show me* for *touch*.

Allowable Verbal Prompt

Touch the apple.

Objective 3

Select own photo or written name

Materials

- Photo of the student
- Photo of a person unfamiliar to the student

Administration Directions

Present the two pictures to the student. Say, **Here is your picture.** Attract attention to the picture of the student by shaking or tapping it. Then say, **This is (student's name). Show me the picture of (student's name).** Allow 5 seconds for the student to initiate a response. Wait as long as it takes for the student to complete the response.

Substitutions

Depending upon the language repertoire and physical ability of the student, substitute the words *look at* or *touch* for *show me*.

Allowable Verbal Prompt

Which one is (student's name)?

Materials

- Photo of the student with the student's name written below it
- Photo of a person unfamiliar to the student

Administration Directions

Present the picture of the student. **Here is your picture and here is your name.** Attract attention to the picture and then the name written at the bottom of the photo. Present the picture of the unfamiliar person. **Here is another picture. Which picture has your name written on it? Show me the picture that has your name written on it.** Allow 5 seconds for the student to initiate a response. Wait as long as it takes for the student to complete the response.

Substitutions

Depending upon the language repertoire and physical ability of the student, substitute the words *look at* or *touch* for *show me*.

Allowable Verbal Prompt

Which picture has your name written on it?

Materials

- Photo of the student
- An index card with the student's name written on it
- An index card with a different name written on it

Administration Directions

Present the student with the index card that has his or her name written on it and the student's photo. Say, **Look. Here is your name and here is your picture. Now I'm going to take away your picture. I want you to find your name.**

Then present the two index cards with the names written on them. Say, **Show me your name.** Allow 5 seconds for the student to initiate a response. Wait as long as it takes for the student to complete the response.

Substitutions

Depending upon the language repertoire and physical ability of the student, substitute the words *look at* or *touch* for *show me*.

Allowable Verbal Prompt

Show me your name.

Objective 4

Select named photo or word

Objective 4: Item 8 • 128

Materials

A red apple

Administration Directions

Present the red apple and the picture of the apple on the student page. While holding up the apple say, **Here is an apple.** Then point to the apple on the student page and say, **Here is a picture of an apple.** Touch the picture of the apple and say, **Show me the picture of the apple.** Allow 5 seconds for the student to initiate a response. Wait as long as it takes for the student to complete the response.

Substitutions

Depending upon the language repertoire and physical ability of the student, substitute the words *look at* or *touch* for *show me*.

Allowable Verbal Prompt

Show me the picture of the apple.

Objective 4: Item 9 • 130

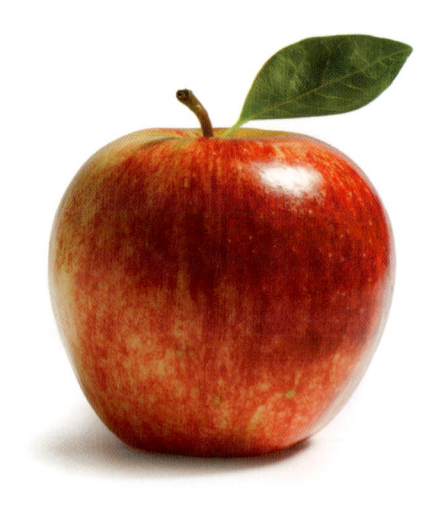

Materials

A red apple

Administration Directions

Present the red apple and the pictures of the apple and the orange on the student page. While holding up the apple say, **Here is an apple.** Then place the apple near the student. Touch the picture of the apple and the orange on the student page and say, **This is an apple** (point to the apple), **and this is an orange** (point to the orange). **Show me the picture of the apple.** Allow 5 seconds for the student to initiate a response. Wait as long as it takes for the student to complete the response.

Substitutions

Depending upon the language repertoire and physical ability of the student, substitute the words *look at* or *touch* for *show me*.

Allowable Verbal Prompt

Show me the picture of the apple.

orange | **apple**

Administration Directions

Present the student page to the student. Then say, **I want you to show me the picture that has the word *apple* written below it.** Allow 5 seconds for the student to initiate a response. Wait as long as it takes for the student to complete the response.

Substitutions

Depending upon the language repertoire and physical ability of the student, substitute the words *look at* or *touch* for *show me*.

Allowable Verbal Prompt

Show me the picture that has the word *apple* written below it.

apple

Administration Directions

Present the student page to the student. Say, **Look, here's the word *apple*** (point to the word), **and here's a picture of an apple** (point to the picture). **Show me the word *apple*.** Allow 5 seconds for the student to initiate a response. Wait as long as it takes for the student to complete the response.

Substitutions

Depending upon the language repertoire and physical ability of the student, substitute the words *look at* or *touch* for *show me*.

Allowable Verbal Prompt

Show me the word *apple*.

apple

potato

Administration Directions

Present the student page to the student. **This is the word *apple*** (point to the word), **and this is the word *potato*** (point to the word). **Show me the word *apple*. These are your two choices. Show me the word *apple*.** Allow 5 seconds for the student to initiate a response. Wait as long as it takes for the student to complete the response.

Substitutions

Depending upon the language repertoire and physical ability of the student, substitute the words *look at* or *touch* for *show me*.

Allowable Verbal Prompt

Show me the word *apple*.

Objective 5

Physically engage with a book and/or visually attend to a story

Materials

Oh My, Apple Pie! easel book

Administration Directions

Present the book and say, **Look, here is our book.** Read up to line 3. Then say, **Look, here is the apple** (point to the picture of the apple). **You touch the picture of the apple.** Allow 5 seconds for the student to initiate a response. Wait as long as it takes for the student to complete the response.

Substitutions

Depending upon the language repertoire and physical ability of the student, substitute the words *look at* or *touch* for *show me*.

Allowable Verbal Prompt

Touch the picture of the apple.

Materials

Oh My, Apple Pie! easel book

Administration Directions

Continue reading the book. Read lines 4 and 5. Then say, **Look, here is Grandma.** Touch the picture of the grandma. **You touch the picture of Grandma.** Allow 5 seconds for the student to initiate a response. Wait as long as it takes for the student to complete the response.

Substitutions

Depending upon the language repertoire and physical ability of the student, substitute the words *look at* or *touch* for *show me*.

Allowable Verbal Prompt

Touch the picture of Grandma.

Materials

Oh My, Apple Pie! easel book

Administration Directions

Continue reading the book. Read line 6. **Look, here is an apple pie.** Touch the picture of the apple pie. **You touch the picture of an apple pie.** Allow 5 seconds for the student to initiate a response. Wait as long as it takes for the student to complete the response.

Substitutions

Depending upon the language repertoire and physical ability of the student, substitute the words *look at* or *touch* for *show me*.

Allowable Verbal Prompt

Touch the picture of the apple pie.

Materials

Oh My, Apple Pie! easel book

Administration Directions

Show the student the cover of the book. Put your finger on the first word (do not move your finger to the other words). **You touch these words as I read. Start here.** Allow 5 seconds for the student to initiate a response. Wait as long as it takes for the student to complete the response.

Substitutions

For students who are unable to touch the words, print the title page from Disc 1 and cut out the words. Space out the words more. Put your finger on the first word (do not move your finger to other words). **Look at these words as I read. Start here.** Observe the student's eye movements if the student uses eye gaze as a response.

Allowable Verbal Prompt

You touch the words on this cover.

Objective 6

Point to an object, a picture, or a word that completes a story line

Oh my, apple pie!

Oh my, apple pie!

Oh my, **apple** pie!

Note: Cover the word *apple* highlighted in yellow on the student page with a Post-it® note. If the student is nonverbal, preprogram an AAC device to say the repeated word.

Materials

- A red apple
- An orange

Administration Directions

Present the apple and orange to the student. Then present the student page. **Look, here I have lines from the story.** Point to the words of the first sentence and emphasize the word *apple* (and also use an AAC device if the student is nonverbal) as you read, **Oh my, apple pie!** Then say, **Listen again.** Point to the words of the second sentence and emphasize the word *apple* (and/or use the AAC device) as you read, **Oh my, apple pie! This time you will finish it.** Then read the third sentence, pointing to the words as you read, pausing at the hidden word. **You finish it.** Allow 5 seconds for the student to initiate a response. Wait as long as it takes for the student to complete the response.

Substitutions

Depending upon the language repertoire and physical ability of the student, substitute the words *look at* or *touch* for *show me*.

Allowable Verbal Prompt

Your turn to finish it.

Oh my, apple pie!
Oh my, apple pie!
Oh my, **apple** pie!

Note: Cover the word *apple* highlighted in yellow on the student page with a Post-it® note. If the student is nonverbal, preprogram an AAC device to say the repeated word.

Administration Directions

Present the student page. **Look, here I have lines from the story again.** Point to the words of the first sentence and emphasize the word *apple* (and also use an AAC device if the student is nonverbal) as you read, **Oh my, apple pie!** Then say, **Listen again.** Point to the words of the second sentence and emphasize the word *apple* (and/or use the AAC device) as you read, **Oh my, apple pie!** Then read the third sentence, pointing to the words as you read, pausing at the hidden word. Uncover the word and point to it. **You finish it. What goes here?** Point to the pictures of the apple and orange. Allow 5 seconds for the student to initiate a response. Wait as long as it takes for the student to complete the response.

Substitutions

Depending upon the language repertoire and physical ability of the student, substitute the words *look at* or *touch* for *show me*.

Allowable Verbal Prompt

Which one? *Apple* or *orange*?

Oh my, apple pie!

Oh my, apple pie!

Oh my, **apple** pie!

| apple | orange |

Note: Cover the word *apple* highlighted in yellow on the student page with a Post-it® note. If the student is nonverbal, preprogram an AAC device to say the repeated word.

Administration Directions

Present the student page. **Look, here I have lines from the story again.** Point to the words of the first sentence and emphasize the word *apple* (and also use an AAC device if the student is nonverbal) as you read, **Oh my, apple pie!** Then say, **Listen again.** Point to the words of the second sentence and emphasize the word *apple* (and/or use the AAC device) as you read, **Oh my, apple pie!** Then read the third sentence, pointing to the words as you read, pausing at the hidden word. Uncover the word and point to it. **What goes here? Apple or orange?** Point to the words. Allow 5 seconds for the student to initiate a response. Wait as long as it takes for the student to complete the response.

Substitutions

Depending upon the language repertoire and physical ability of the student, substitute the words *look at* or *touch* for *show me*.

Allowable Verbal Prompt

Which one? *Apple* or *orange?*

Objective 7

Respond to literal questions about a story

pencil

apple

Materials

Oh My, Apple Pie! easel book

Administration Directions

Display the Oh My, Apple Pie! easel book so the student can see it. While you read the story, drag your finger along below the words. Ask the questions immediately after reading the line where the answer appears.

What kind of pie does Lisa's grandma make? Was it apple or pencil? (Line 3)

Present the student page. Allow 5 seconds for the student to initiate a response. Wait as long as it takes for the student to complete the response.

Substitutions

Depending upon the language repertoire and physical ability of the student, use the words *look at, show me,* or *touch.*

Allowable Verbal Prompt

Repeat the question.

nose

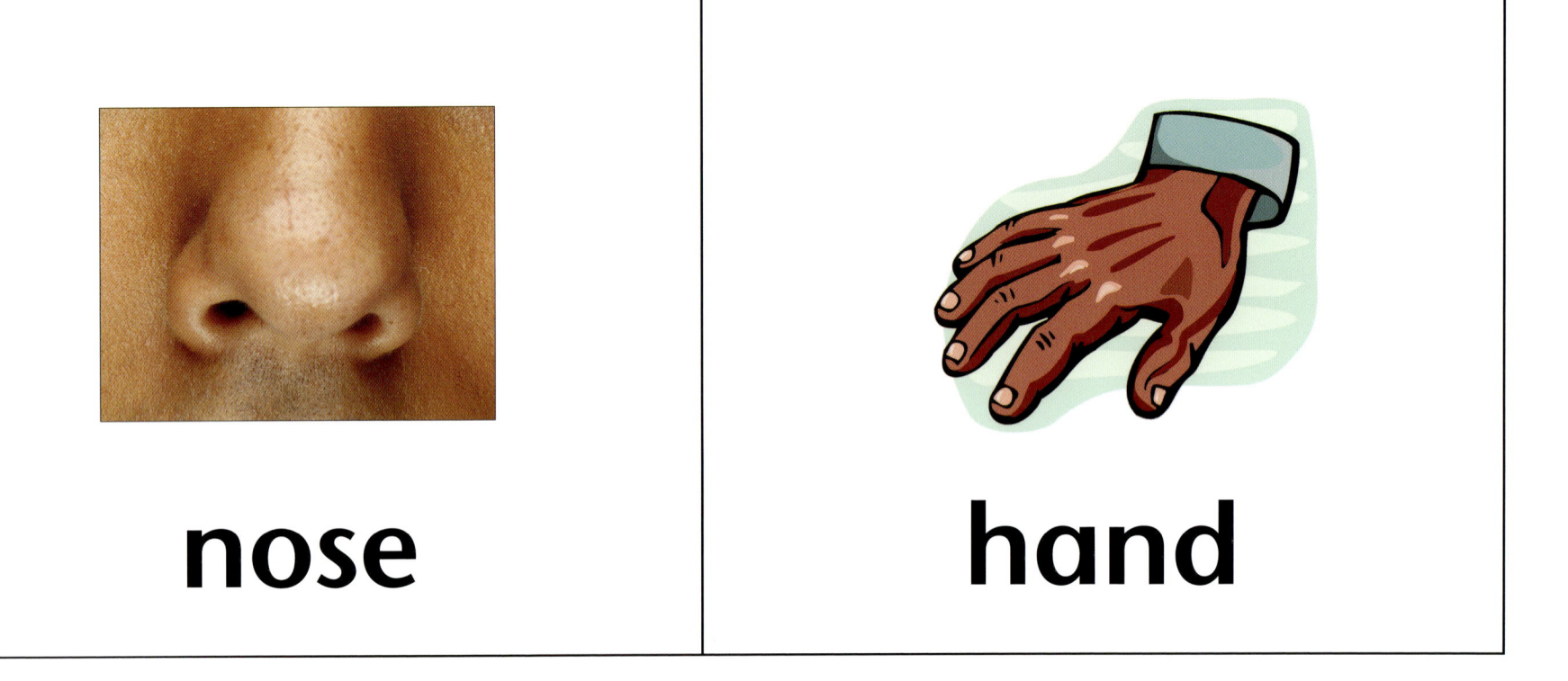

hand

Materials

Oh My, Apple Pie! easel book

Administration Directions

Display the Oh My, Apple Pie! easel book so the student can see it. While you read the story, drag your finger along below the words. Ask the question immediately after reading the line where the answer appears.

Will the scent of apple pie fill Lisa's nose or her hand? (Line 5)

Present the student page. Allow 5 seconds for the student to initiate a response. Wait as long as it takes for the student to complete the response.

Substitutions

Depending upon the language repertoire and physical ability of the student, use the words *look at, show me,* or *touch.*

Allowable Verbal Prompt

Repeat the question.

play

eat dinner

Materials

Oh My, Apple Pie! easel book

Administration Directions

Display the Oh My, Apple Pie! easel book so the student can see it. While you read the story, drag your finger along below the words. Ask the questions immediately after reading the line where the answer appears.

What must Lisa do before she gets apple pie? Play or eat dinner? (Line 9)

Present the student page. Allow 5 seconds for the student to initiate a response. Wait as long as it takes for the student to complete the response.

Substitutions

Depending upon the language repertoire and physical ability of the student, use the words *look at, show me,* or *touch.*

Allowable Verbal Prompt

Repeat the question.

kiss

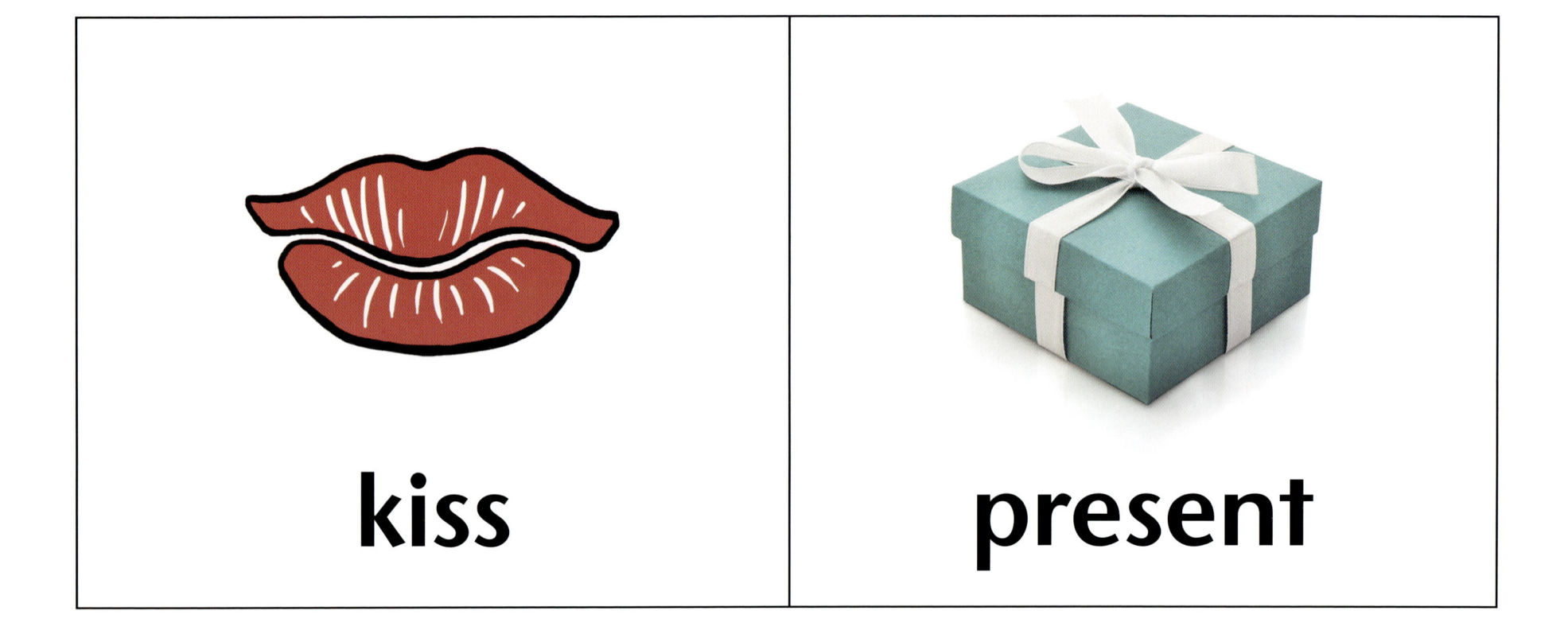

present

Materials

Oh My, Apple Pie! easel book

Administration Directions

Display the Oh My, Apple Pie! easel book so the student can see it. While you read the story, drag your finger along below the words. Ask the question immediately after reading the line where the answer appears.

What did Lisa's pie come with? A kiss or a present? (Line 19)

Present the student page. Allow 5 seconds for the student to initiate a response. Wait as long as it takes for the student to complete the response.

Substitutions

Depending upon the language repertoire and physical ability of the student, use the words *look at, show me,* or *touch.*

Allowable Verbal Prompt

Repeat the question.

banana

apple

Materials

Oh My, Apple Pie! easel book

Administration Directions

Display the Oh My, Apple Pie! easel book so the student can see it. While you read the story, drag your finger along below the words. Ask the question immediately after reading the line where the answer appears.

What kind of pie was our book about?
(Line 20)

Present the student page. Allow 5 seconds for the student to initiate a response. Wait as long as it takes for the student to complete the response.

Substitutions

Depending upon the language repertoire and physical ability of the student, use the words *look at, show me,* or *touch.*

Allowable Verbal Prompt

Repeat the question.

Objective 8

Point to named objects or pictures

Materials

- A red apple
- A sock (or same distractor used when teaching)

Administration Directions

Show the student the red apple and say, **Here is an apple.** Then show the student the sock and say, **Here is a sock. Which one is the apple?** Allow 5 seconds for the student to initiate a response. Wait as long as it takes for the student to complete the response.

Substitutions

Depending upon the language repertoire and physical ability of the student, substitute the words *look at, show me,* or *touch.*

Allowable Verbal Prompt

Which one is the apple?

Objective 8: Item 26 • 164

Administration Directions

Show the student the picture of the apple in the story and say, **Here is an apple.** Then point to the pictures and say, **Which one is the apple?** Allow 5 seconds for the student to initiate a response. Wait as long as it takes for the student to complete the response.

Substitutions

Depending upon the language repertoire and physical ability of the student, substitute the words *look at, show me,* or *touch.*

Allowable Verbal Prompt

Which one is the apple?

Objective 8: Item 27 • 166

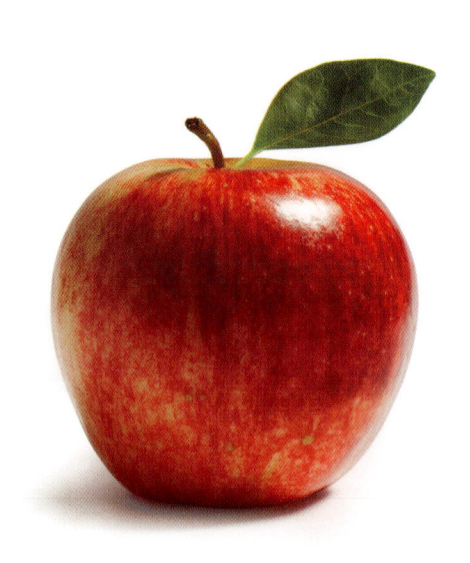

Administration Directions

Present the student page and say, **Here is a sock** (while pointing to the sock), **and here is an apple** (while pointing to the apple). **Which one is the apple?** Allow 5 seconds for the student to initiate a response. Wait as long as it takes for the student to complete the response.

Substitutions

Depending upon the language repertoire and physical ability of the student, substitute the words *look at, show me,* or *touch.*

Allowable Verbal Prompt

Which one is the apple?

Objective 8: Item 28 • 168

Administration Directions

Present the student page and say, **Here is a banana** (while pointing to the banana), **and here is an apple** (while pointing to the apple). **Which one is the apple?** Allow 5 seconds for the student to initiate a response. Wait as long as it takes for the student to complete the response.

Substitutions

Depending upon the language repertoire and physical ability of the student, substitute the words *look at, show me,* or *touch.*

Allowable Verbal Prompt

Which one is the apple?

Grandma | **book**

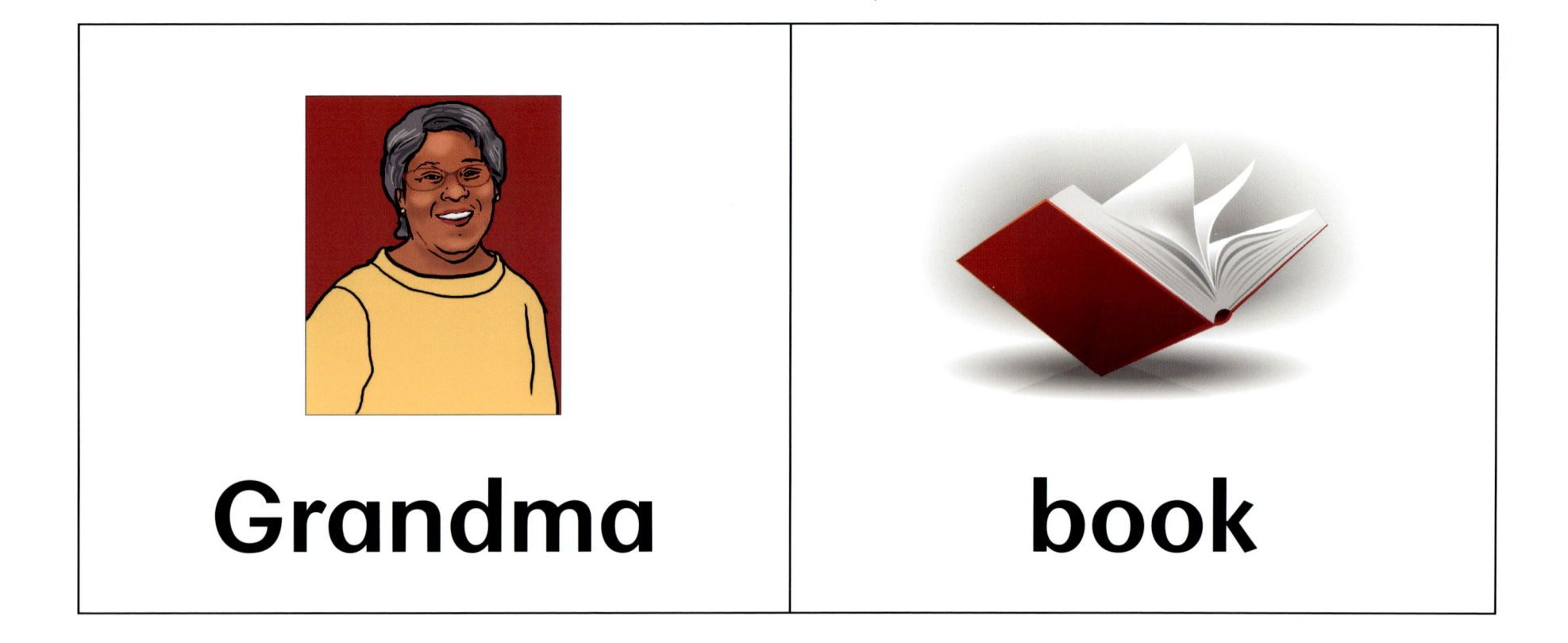

Administration Directions

Present the student page and say, **Here is Grandma** (while pointing to the grandma), **and here is a book** (while pointing to the book). **Which one is Grandma?** Allow 5 seconds for the student to initiate a response. Wait as long as it takes for the student to complete the response.

Substitutions

Depending upon the language repertoire and physical ability of the student, substitute the words *look at, show me,* or *touch.*

Allowable Verbal Prompt

Which one is Grandma?

sock

apple pie

Administration Directions

Present the student page and say, **Here is a sock** (while pointing to the sock), **and here is an apple pie** (while pointing to the apple pie). **Which one is the apple pie?** Allow 5 seconds for the student to initiate a response. Wait as long as it takes for the student to complete the response.

Substitutions

Depending upon the language repertoire and physical ability of the student, substitute the words *look at, show me,* or *touch.*

Allowable Verbal Prompt

Which one is the apple pie?